Jazz Ballads

By Jeff Arnold

ISBN-13: 978-1-4234-0587-0
ISBN-10: 1-4234-0587-0

Hal•Leonard® CORPORATION
7777 W. BLUEMOUND RD. P.O. BOX 13819 MILWAUKEE, WI 53213

Blame It on My Youth

Words by Edward Heyman
Music by Oscar Levant

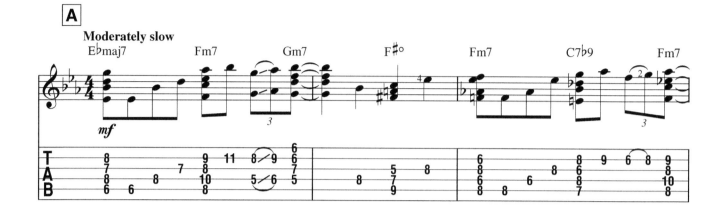

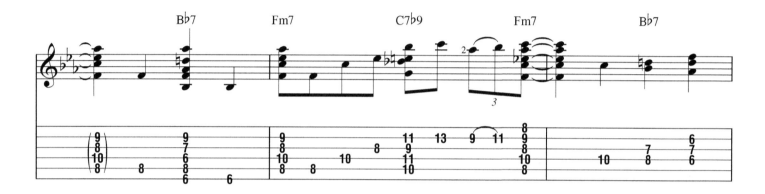

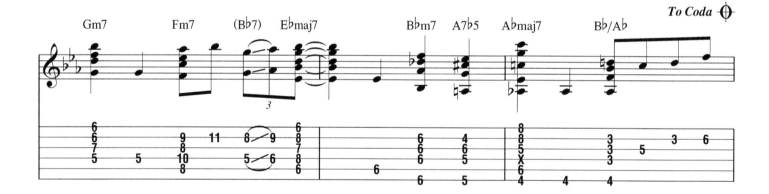

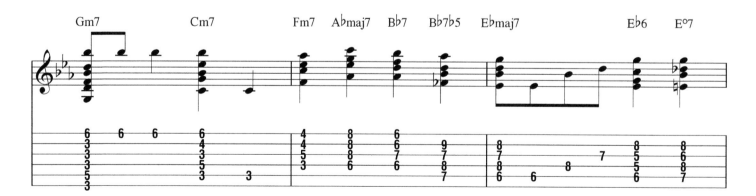

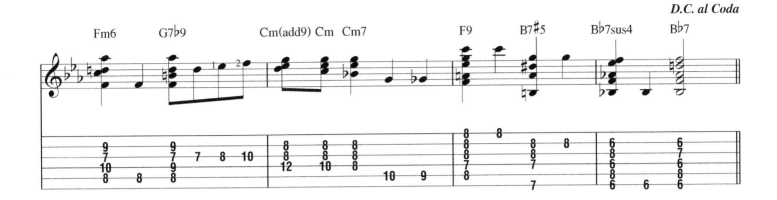

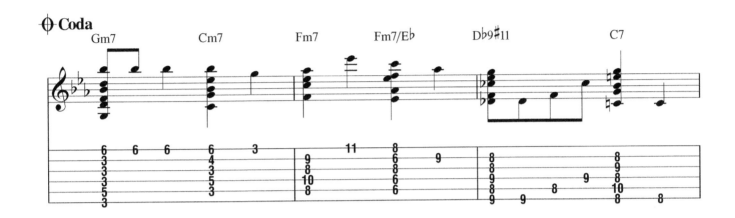

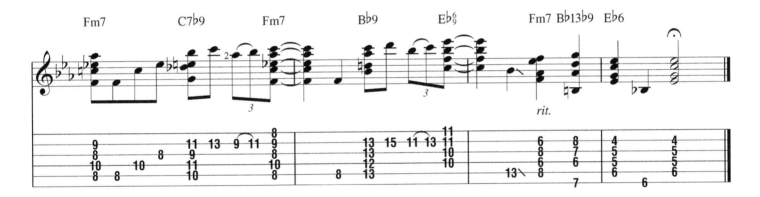

Body and Soul

Words by Edward Heyman, Robert Sour and Frank Eyton
Music by John Green

Darn That Dream

Lyric by Eddie De Lange
Music by Jimmy Van Heusen

But Beautiful

Words by Johnny Burke
Music by Jimmy Van Heusen

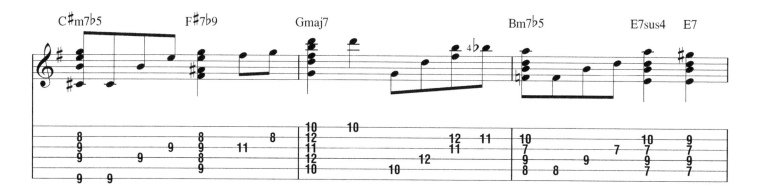

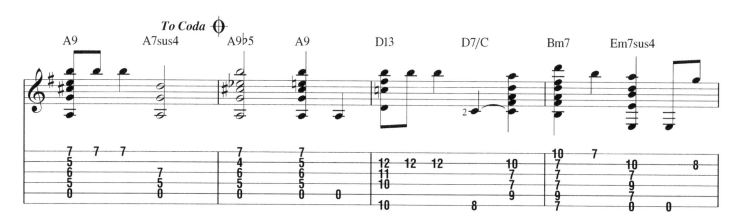

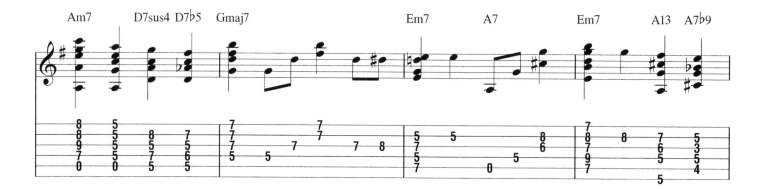

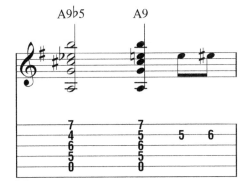

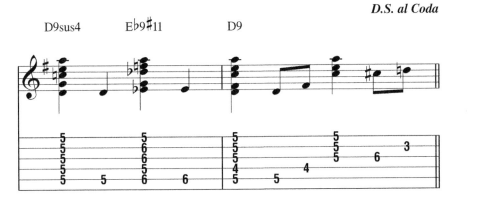

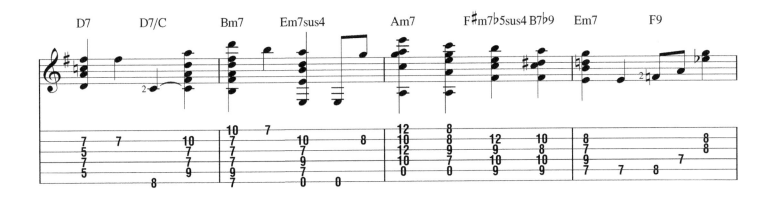

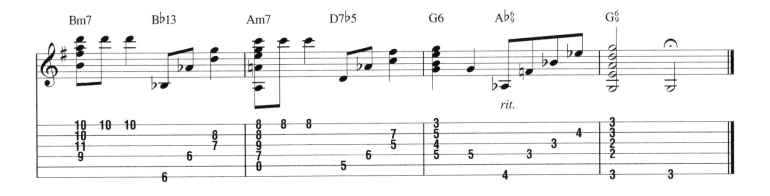

Easy Living

Theme from the Paramount Picture EASY LIVING
Words and Music by Leo Robin and Ralph Rainger

Easy to Love
(You'd Be So Easy to Love)
from BORN TO DANCE
Words and Music by Cole Porter

9

Here's That Rainy Day

Words by Johnny Burke
Music by Jimmy Van Heusen

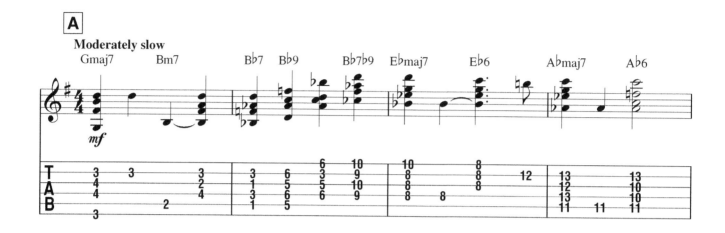

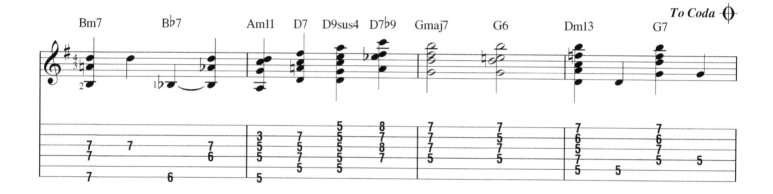

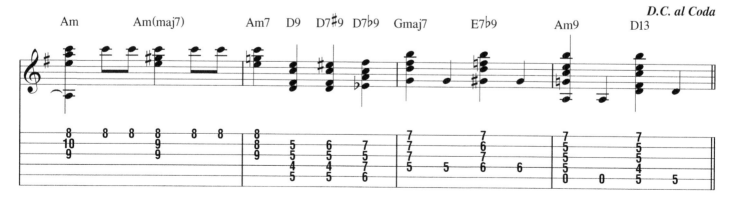

⊕ Coda

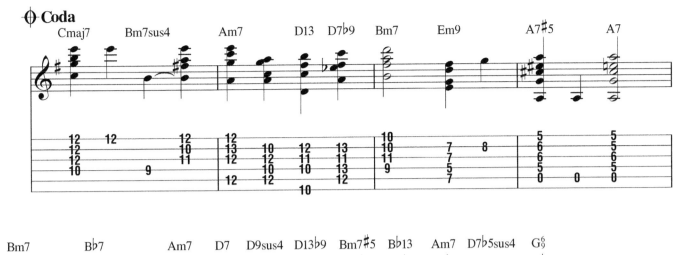

I Could Write a Book

from PAL JOEY

Words by Lorenz Hart
Music by Richard Rodgers

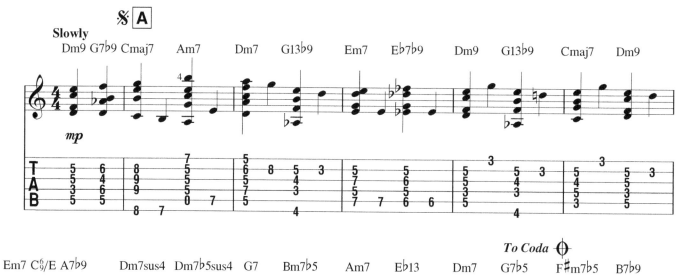

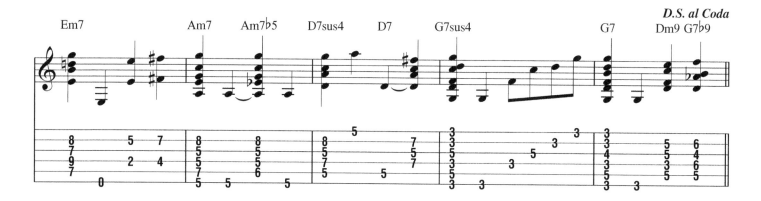

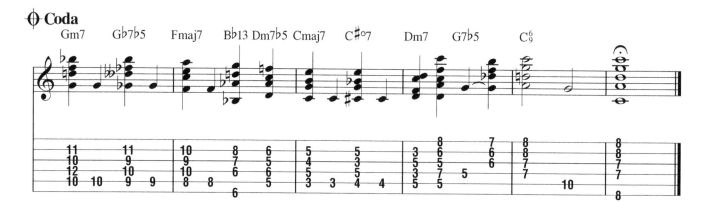

In a Sentimental Mood

By Duke Ellington

13

Long Ago (And Far Away)

from COVER GIRL

Words by Ira Gershwin
Music by Jerome Kern

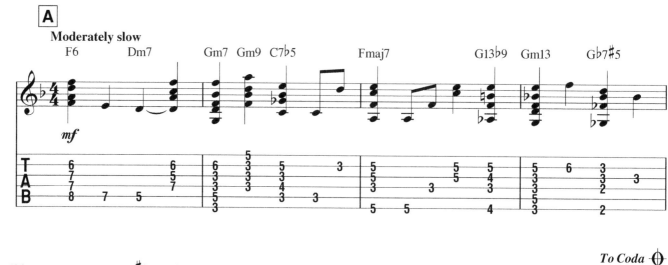

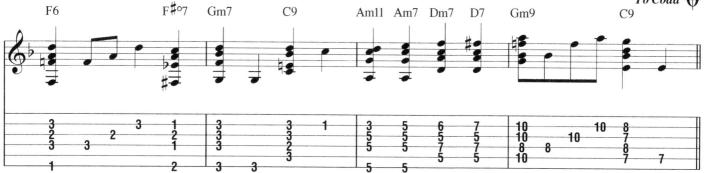

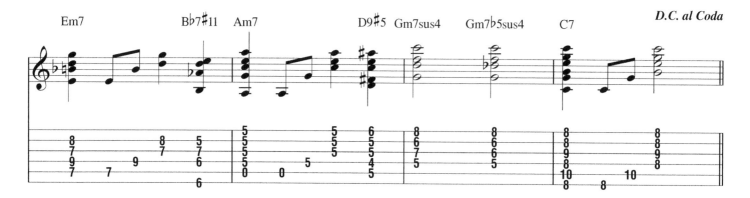

Coda

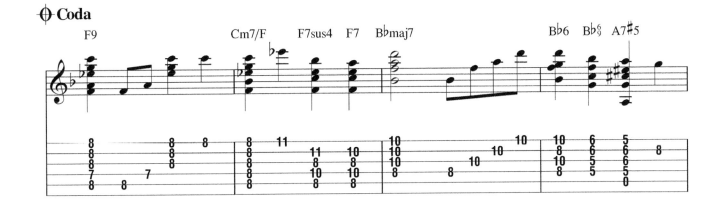

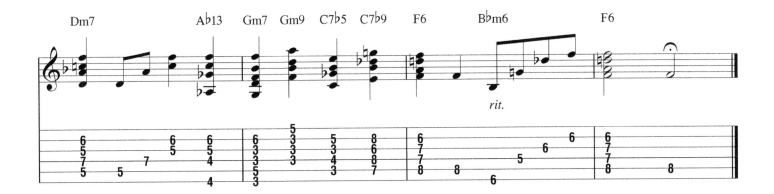

Lover Man

(Oh, Where Can You Be?)

By Jimmy Davis, Roger Ramirez and Jimmy Sherman

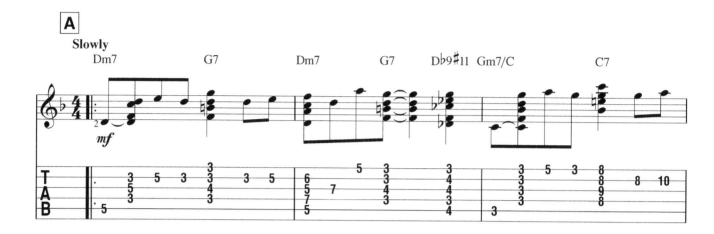

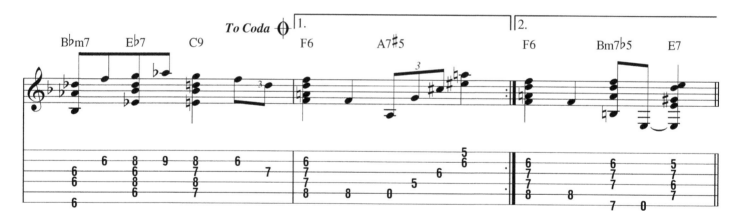

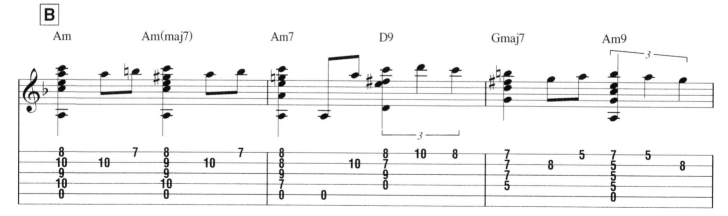

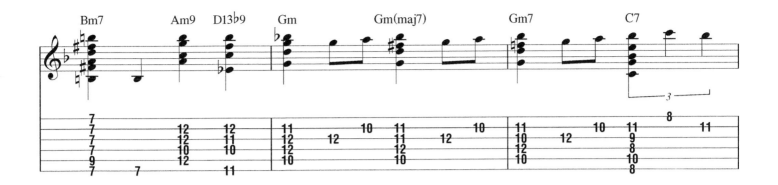

D.C. al Coda

⊕ **Coda**

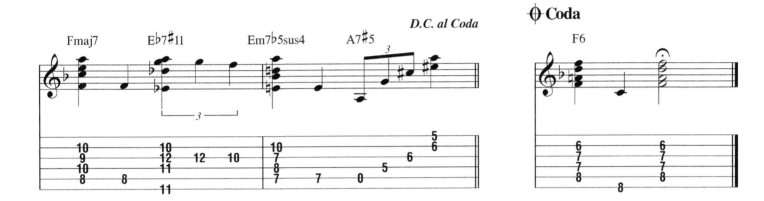

Misty

Music by Erroll Garner

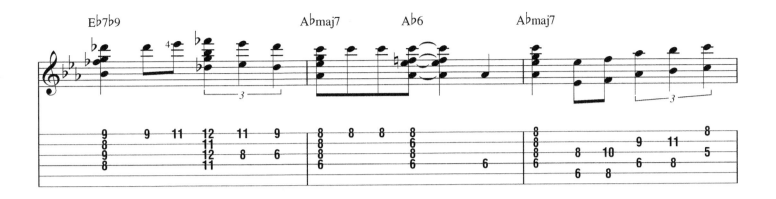

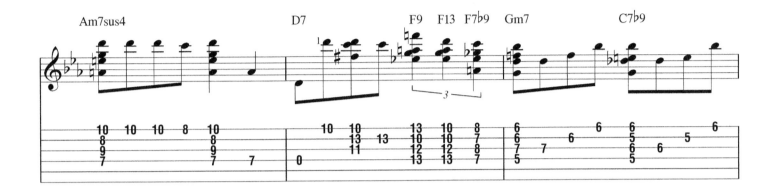

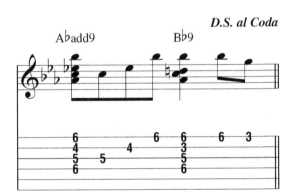

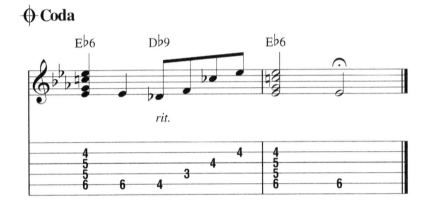

Moonlight in Vermont

Words by John Blackburn
Music by Karl Suessdorf

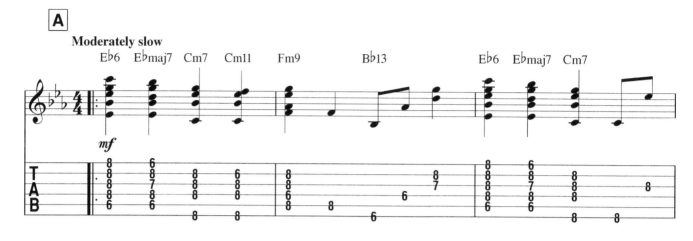

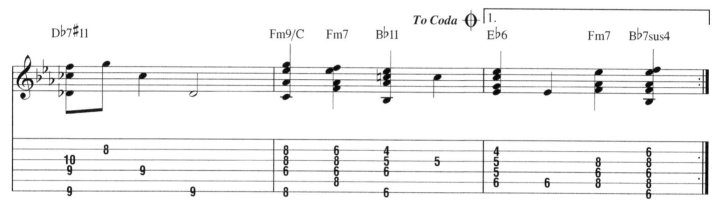

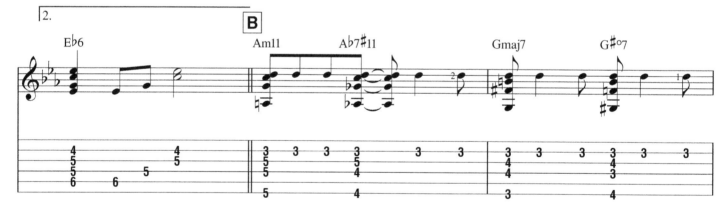

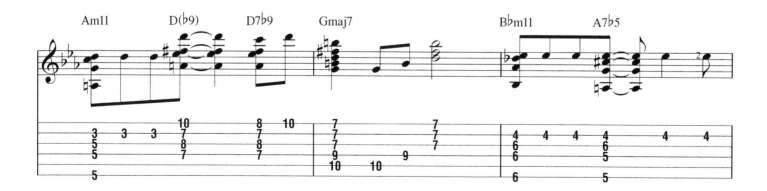

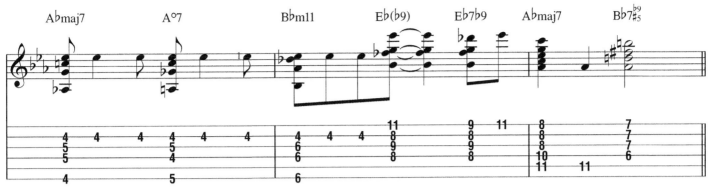

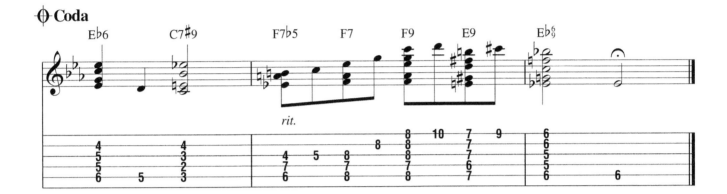

My Foolish Heart

from MY FOOLISH HEART

Words by Ned Washington
Music by Victor Young

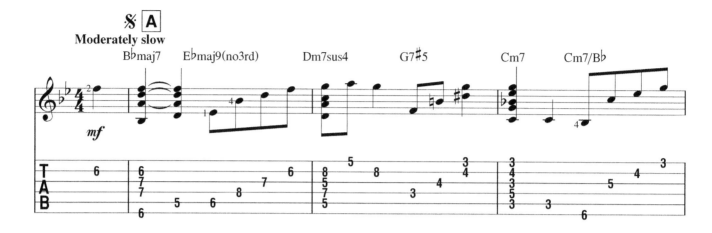

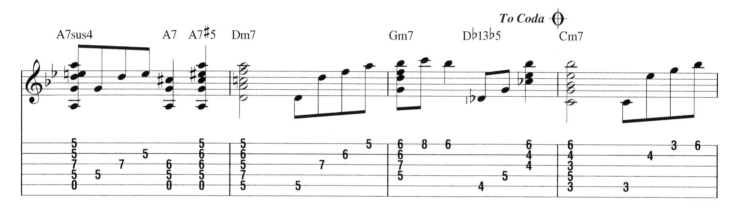

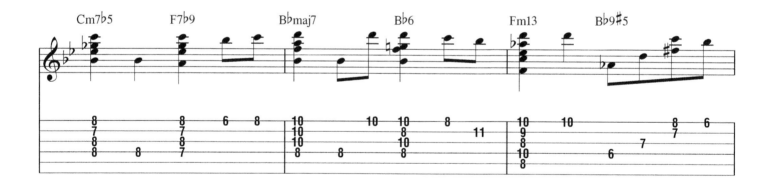

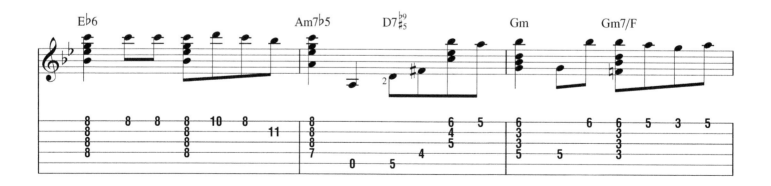

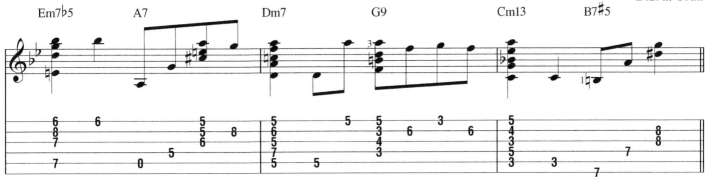

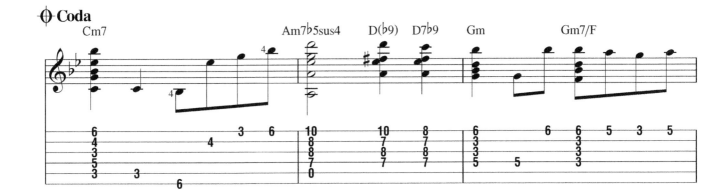

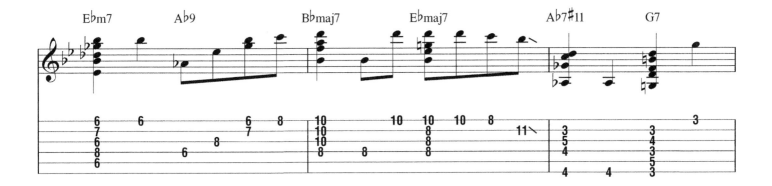

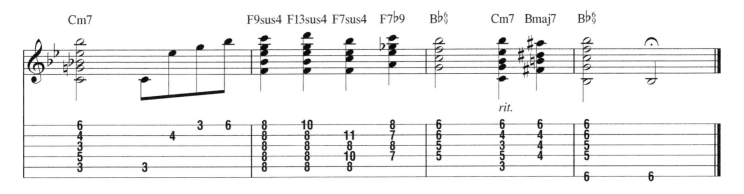

My Funny Valentine

from BABES IN ARMS

Words by Lorenz Hart
Music by Richard Rodgers

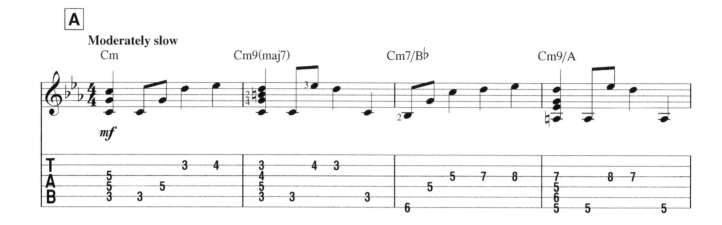

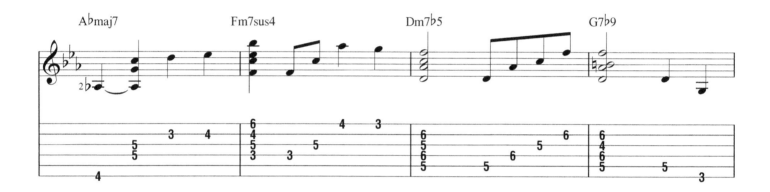

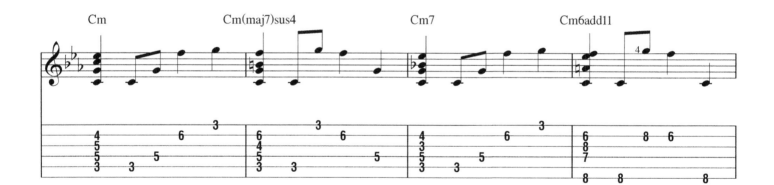

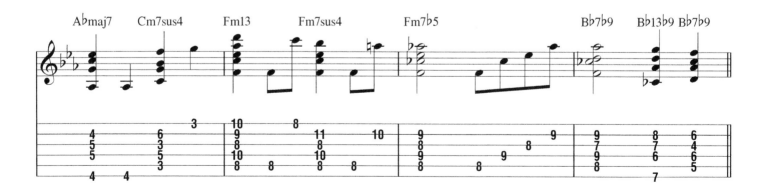

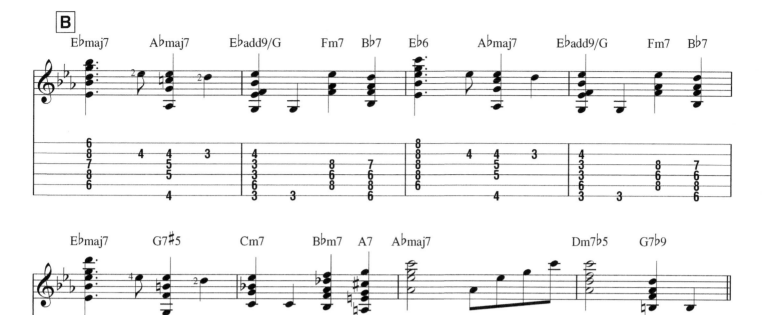

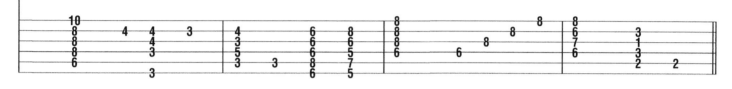

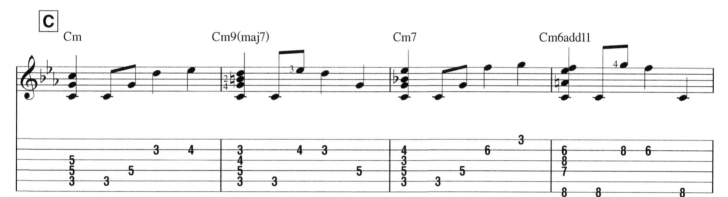

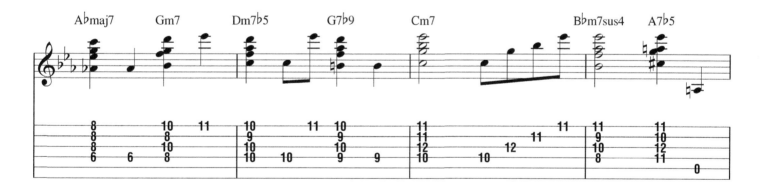

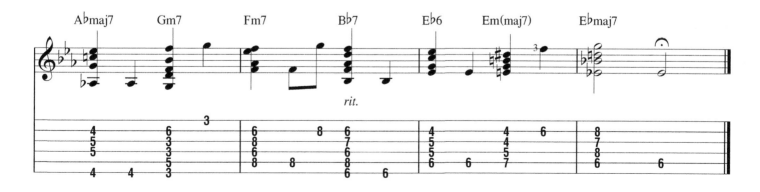

My One and Only Love

Words by Robert Mellin
Music by Guy Wood

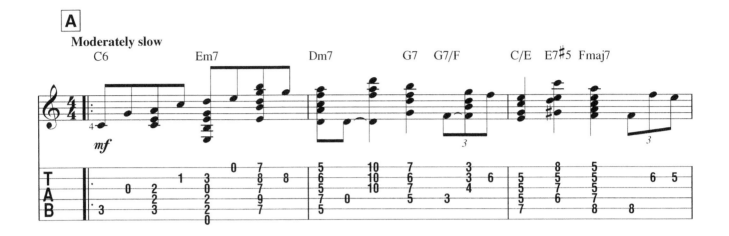

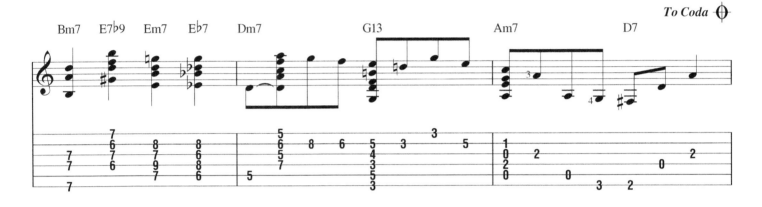

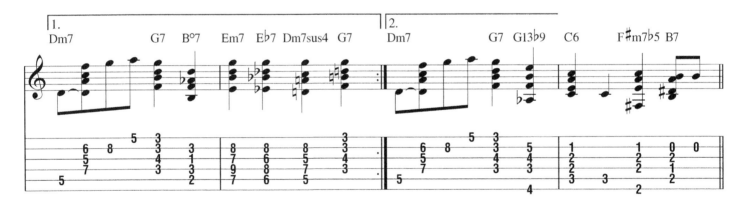

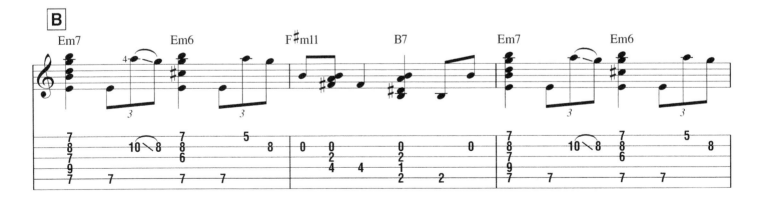

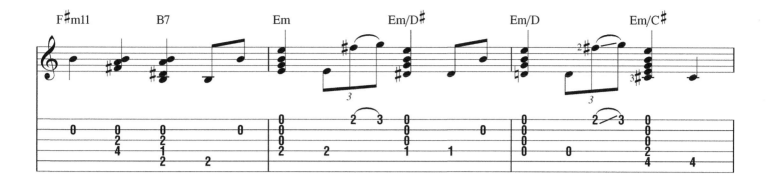

Coda

D.C. al Coda

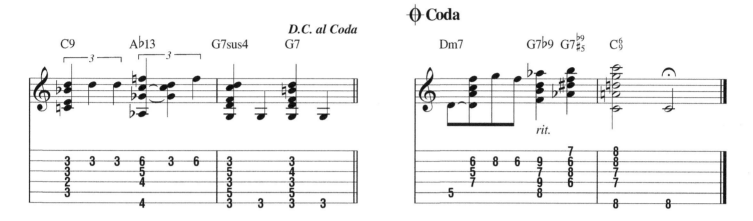

Nancy – With the Laughing Face

Words by Phil Silvers
Music by James Van Heusen

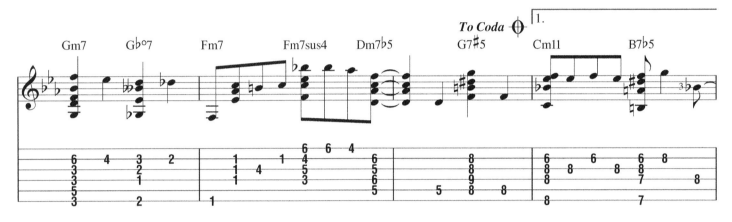

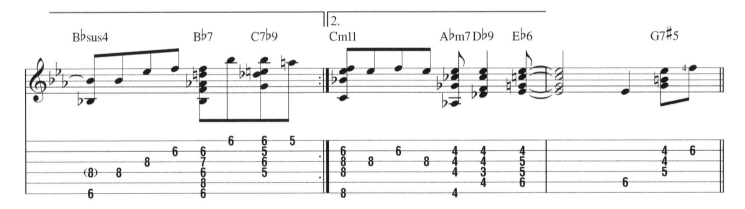

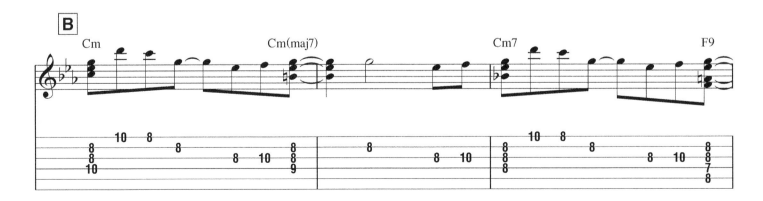

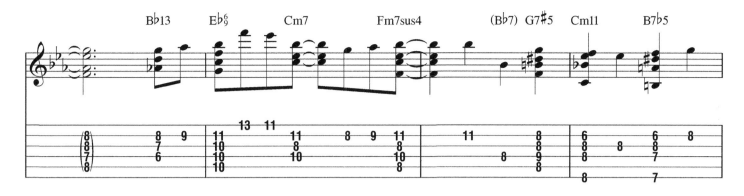

Coda

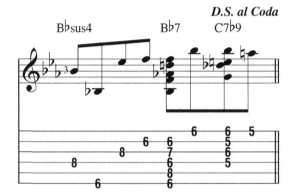

The Nearness of You

from the Paramount Picture ROMANCE IN THE DARK

Words by Ned Washington
Music by Hoagy Carmichael

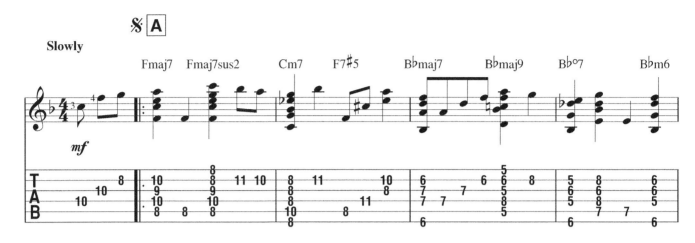

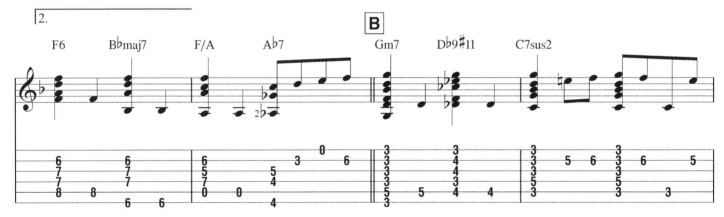

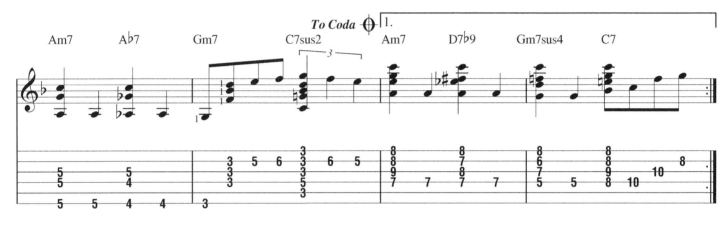

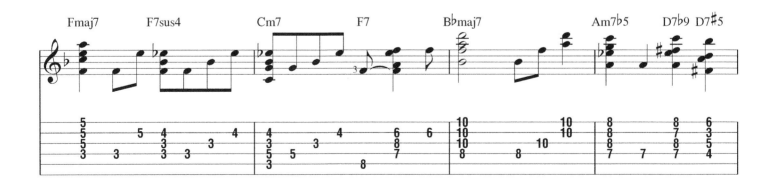

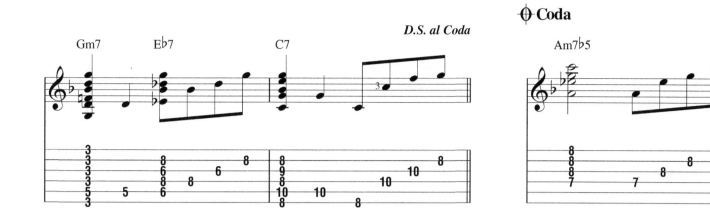

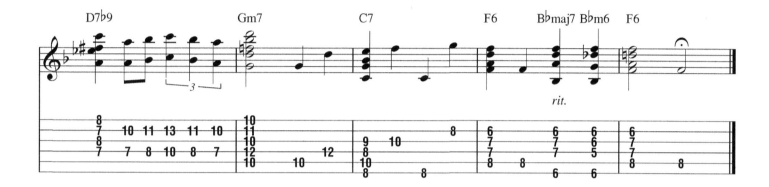

A Nightingale Sang in Berkeley Square

Lyric by Eric Maschwitz
Music by Manning Sherwin

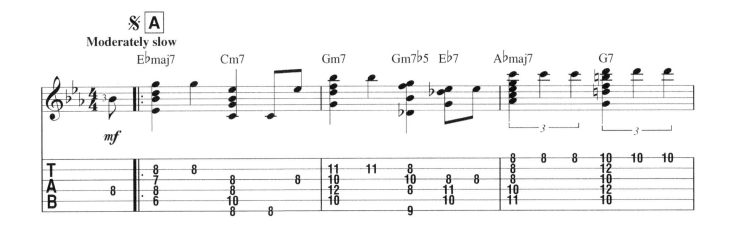

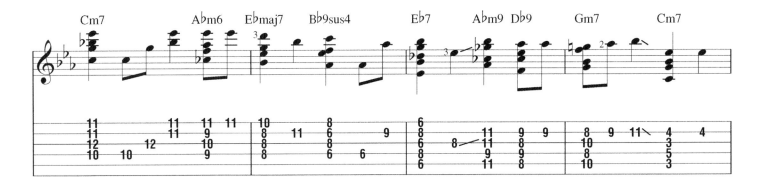

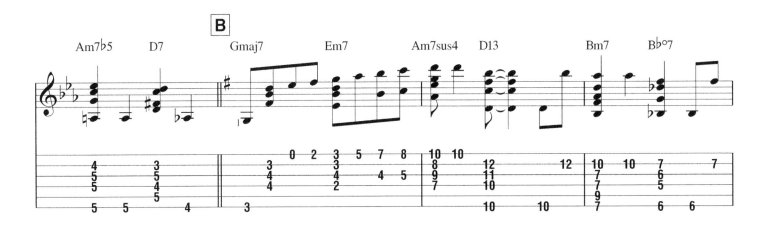

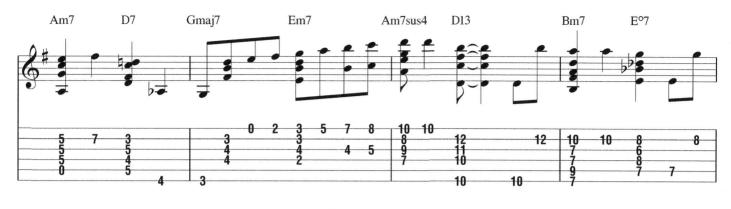

D.S. al Coda

⊕ **Coda**

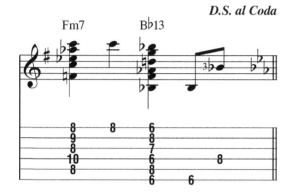

Skylark

Words by Johnny Mercer
Music by Hoagy Carmichael

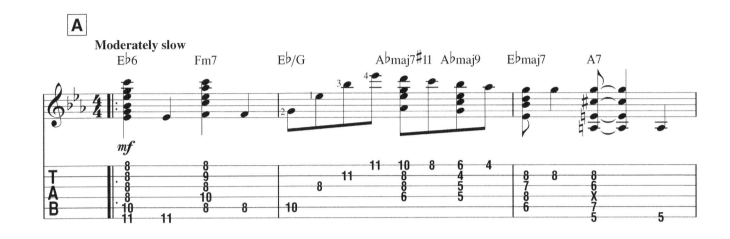

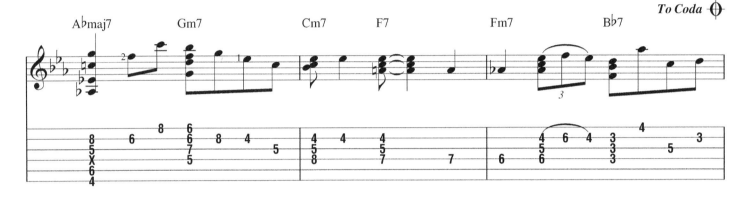

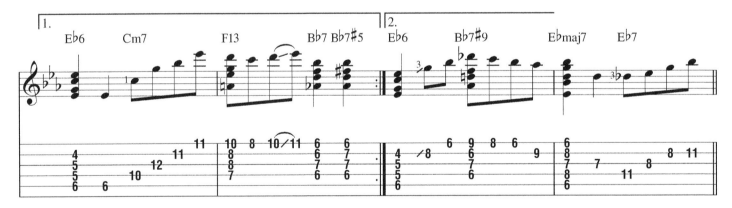

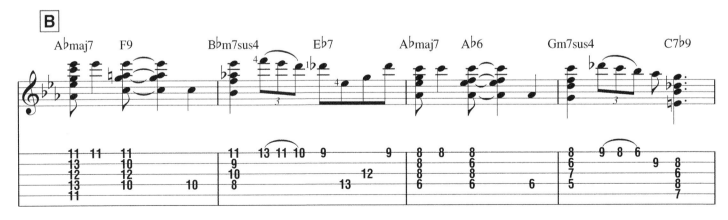

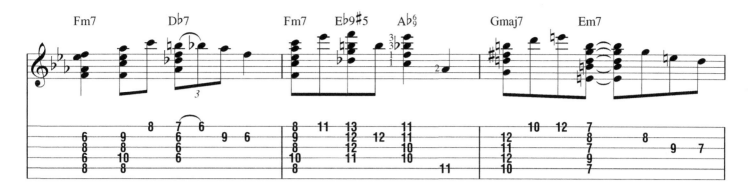

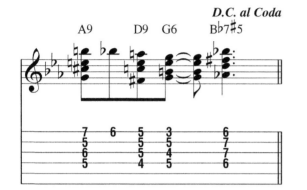

⊕ **Coda**

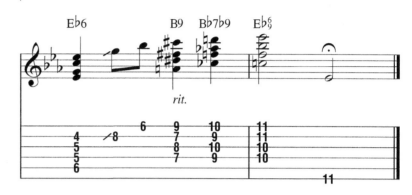

Stella by Starlight

from the Paramount Picture THE UNINVITED

Words by Ned Washington
Music by Victor Young

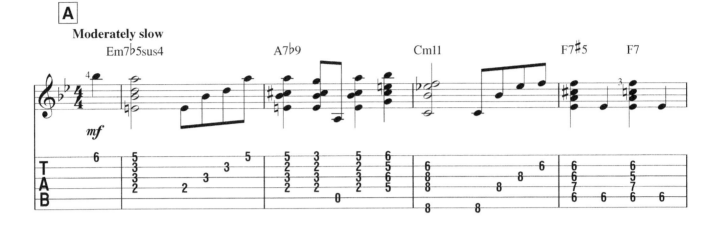

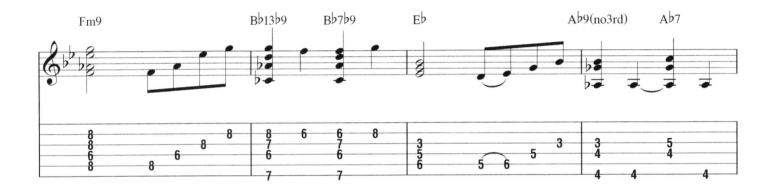

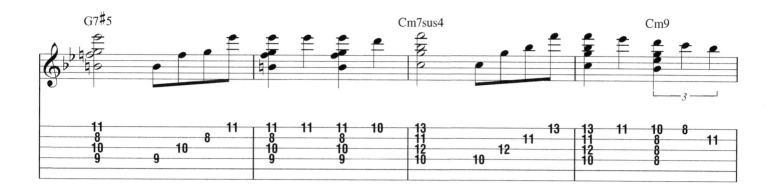

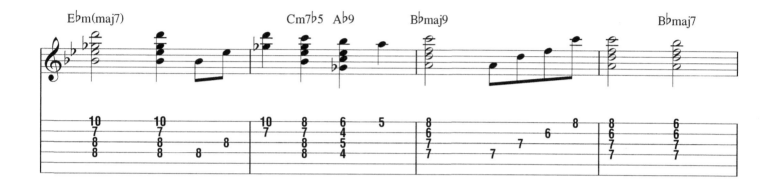

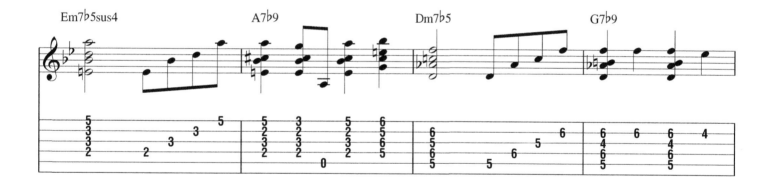

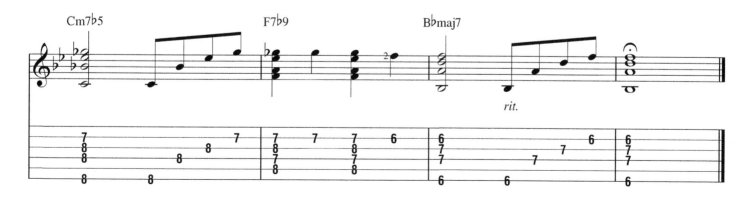

Time After Time

from the Metro-Goldwyn-Mayer Picture IT HAPPENED IN BROOKLYN

Words by Sammy Cahn
Music by Jule Styne

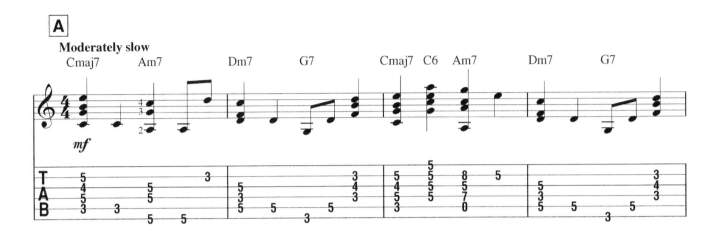

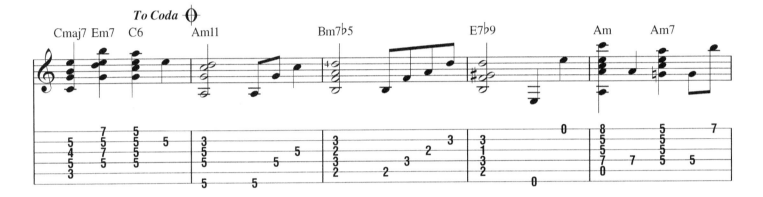

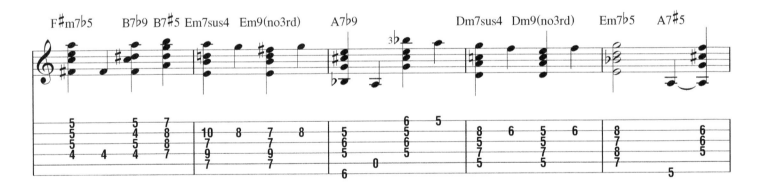

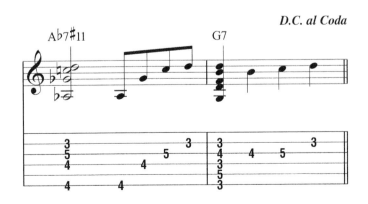

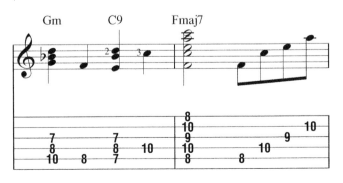

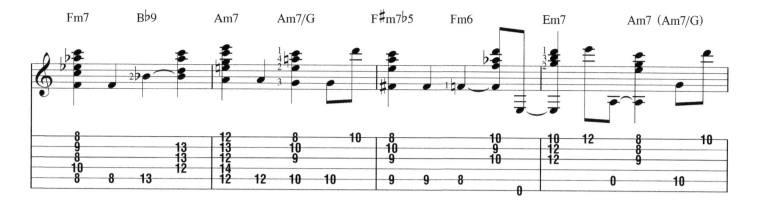

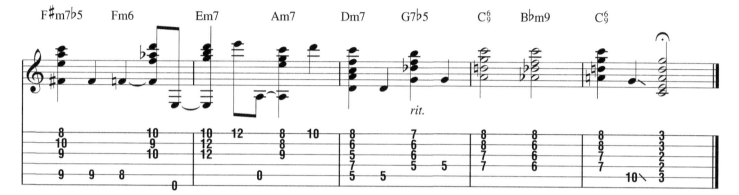

The Very Thought of You

Words and Music by Ray Noble

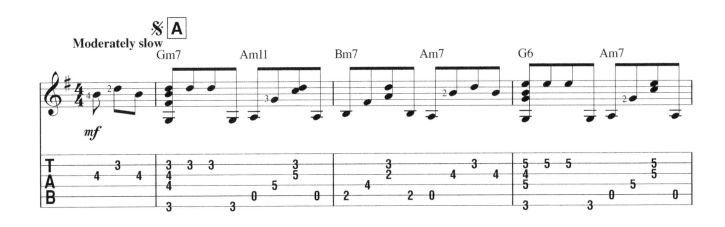

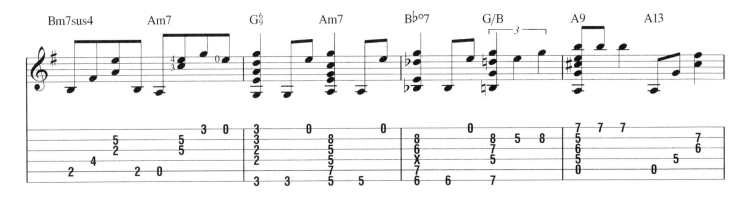

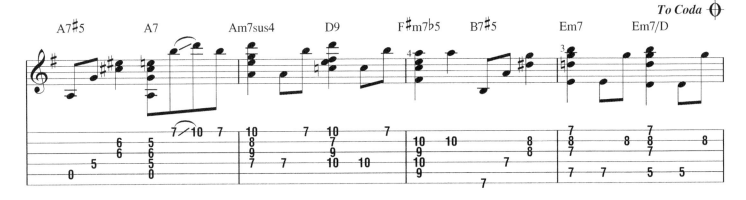

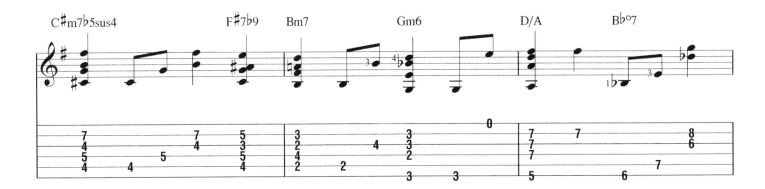

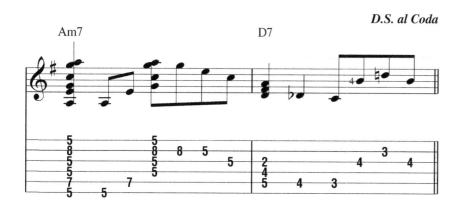

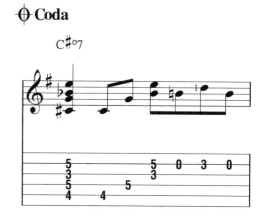

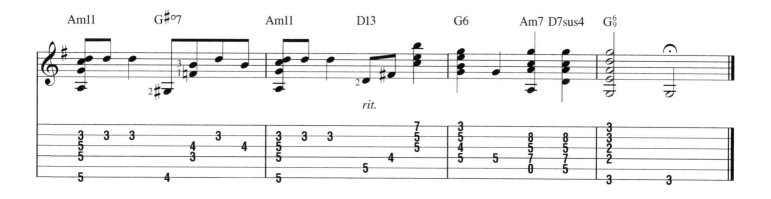

The Way You Look Tonight

from SWING TIME

Words by Dorothy Fields
Music by Jerome Kern

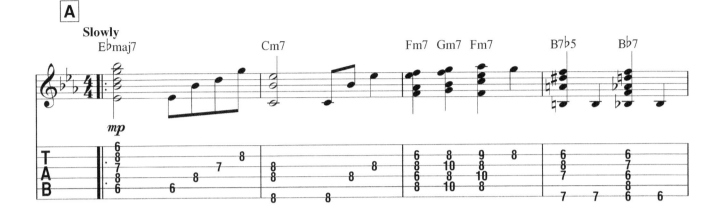

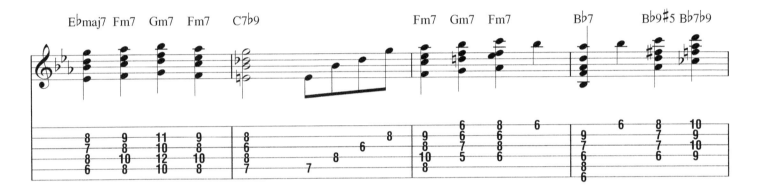

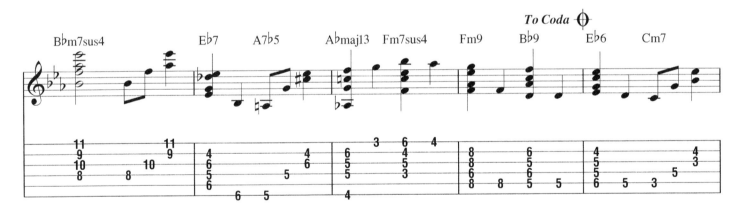

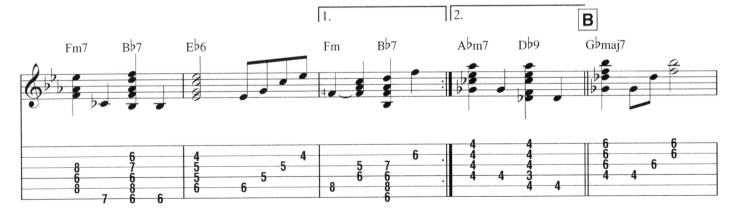

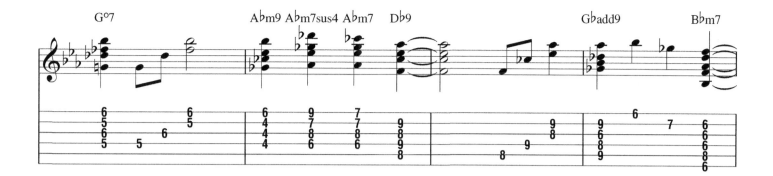

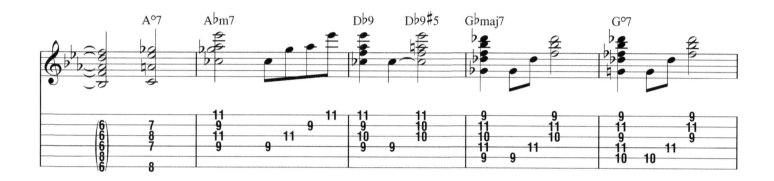

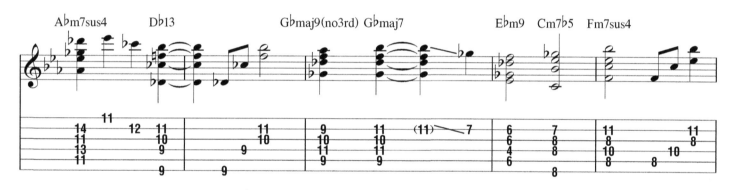

✦ Coda

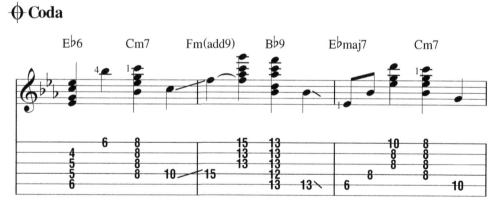

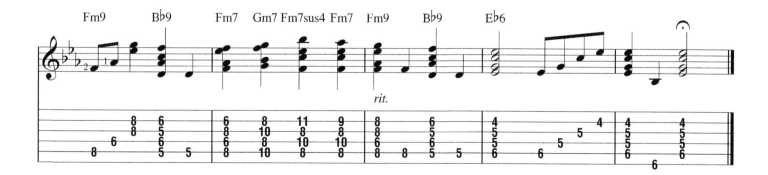

When I Fall in Love

from ONE MINUTE TO ZERO

Words by Edward Heyman
Music by Victor Young

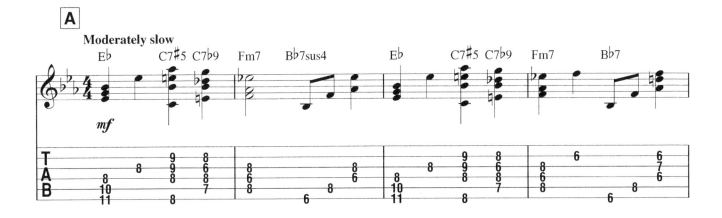

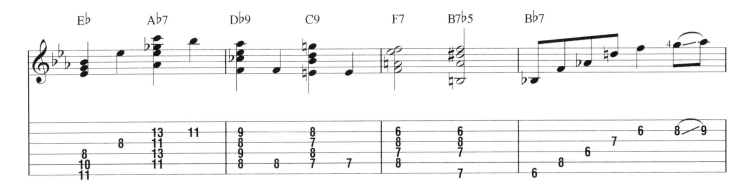

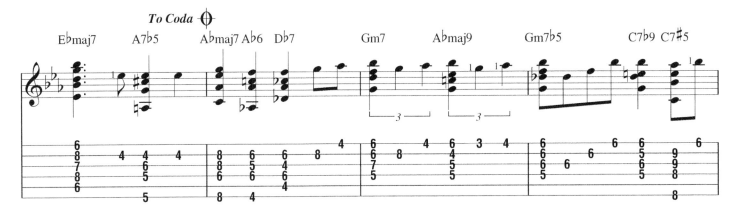

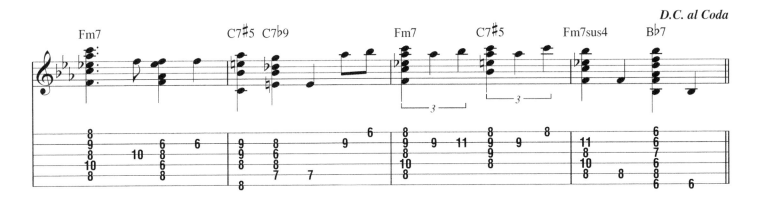

Coda

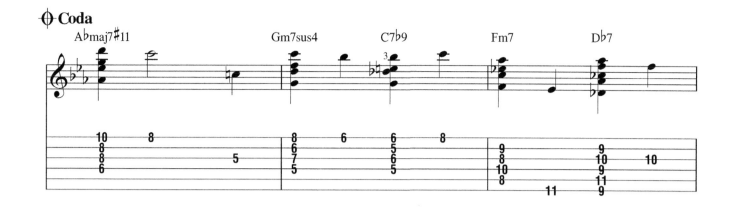

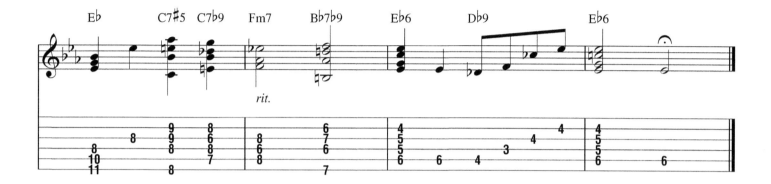

When Sunny Gets Blue

Lyric by Jack Segal
Music by Marvin Fisher

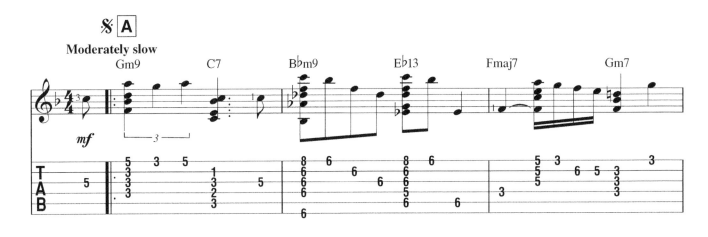

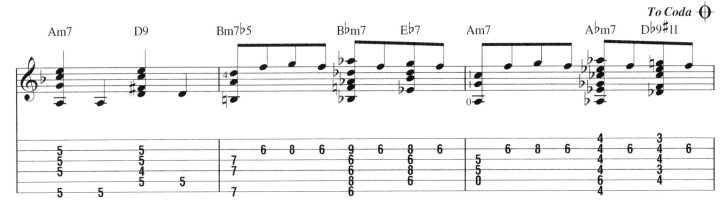

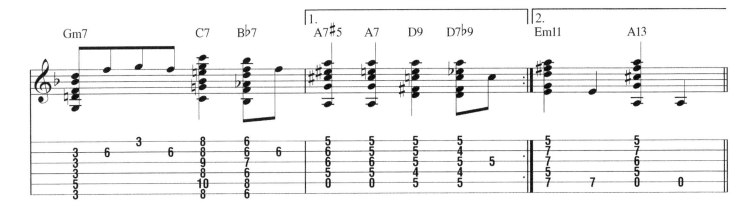

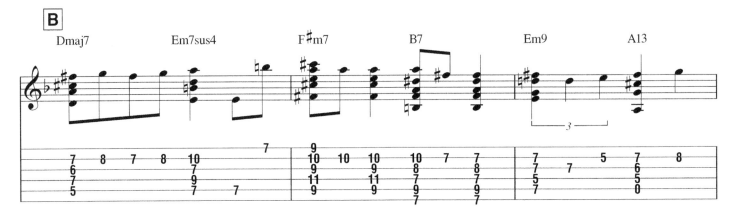

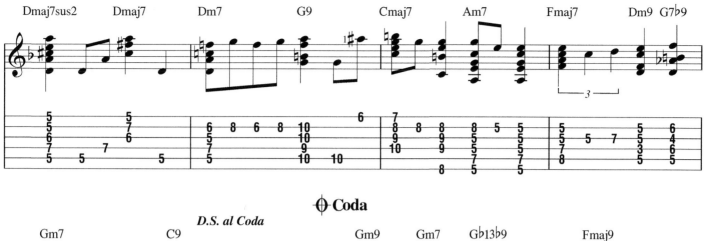

D.S. al Coda

⊕ **Coda**

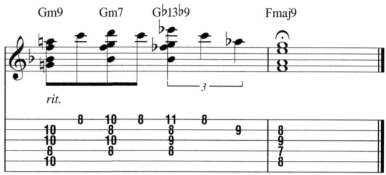

In the Wee Small Hours of the Morning

Words by Bob Hilliard
Music by David Mann